Inspired to Learn

WHY WE MUST GIVE CHILDREN HOPE

Stephen G. Peters

Inspired to Learn

WHY WE MUST GIVE CHILDREN HOPE

Stephen G. Peters

FIRST EDITION 2001

Inspired to Learn:
Why We Must Give Children Hope

Library of Congress Control Number: 2001094643

ISBN 1-880463-08-3
Copyright © 2001 Stephen G. Peters
Copyright © 2001 Rising Sun Publishing, Inc.

P.O. Box 70906
Marietta, GA 30007-0907
(800) 524-2813
info@rspublishing.com
web site: http://www.rspublishing.com

Printed in the United States of America.

Acknowledgments

I thank my family for inspiring me to use my talents wisely and for the benefit of others; Kimberly for your prayers and the opportunity and freedom to do what God has called me to do; my daughters Jillian and Jourdan for their unconditional love and respect; my father, Nathaniel, for being the man he is; my brothers, Ron and Edward; my sisters, Jennifer and Gale; and the parents, teachers, and community members who are fighting so desperately to save this generation and those to come. I thank God for the opportunity to share my experiences with the world; the people of Salisbury, Maryland, for welcoming me into your wonderful community; William "Bill" Middleton for bringing me here; and Rising Sun Publishing for their belief in my message.

Contributors

A special thanks to my editor, Denise Mitchell Smith, who miraculously turned my manuscript into a book and to Laurie Lowe Sorrells who proofread the final copy. And special thanks to Debbie Smith, Verdonda Wright, Susan Bechtol, Janet Benamati, Brian Curtis, Bev Elzey, Cathy Townsend, Nina Wynn, Shannon Holland, Jim King, Ako Kambon, and to Bishop B. Courtney McBath & Pastor Janeen McBath of Calvary Revival Church.

Dedication

This book is dedicated to all our young children who wait daily for us to "switch on" their dreams and to thousands of wonderful and brilliant public educators who truly understand that failure is not an option.

In memory of my dear mother, Charity; grandmother, Adrianna; and brother, Clint. May you rest in peace and know we are all working within the framework of divine purpose.

Contents

About the author

Steve Peters has been a classroom teacher at a Virginia Blue Ribbon School, Assistant principal at a National Blue Ribbon School, and principal of a Virginia Blue Ribbon School.

Mr. Peters, while serving as principal, led the 1100 student Lafayette-Winona Middle School, once marred by violence and tragically low test scores, into recognition as a Virginia Blue Ribbon School. Through a partnership with teachers and the school community Mr. Peters and his team conceptualized effective intervention strategies like "The Gentlemen's Club," as a means of capturing children, inspiring their dreams, and giving them hope.

Inspiring children to learn is not a new concept but an age-old truth. "Capture them, inspire them, and teach them." Mr. Peters has shared his practical strategies, philosophies, beliefs, and message of hope with organizations and school districts throughout the United States and has been featured on such television programs as the Oprah Winfrey Show, and "America, America."

Foreword

Stephen Peters frequently recalls the story of a child perceived to be disadvantaged in more ways than one. Born November 22, 1962, Cleo grew up in rural poverty, but inspired by his mother, he rejected the stigmatizing labels of his school system, which would have had him believe he was less than other students. Today, as a member of Congress, one of his goals is to eliminate the entire system of labeling. Cleo Fields was elected to the Louisiana State Senate at the age of twenty-four, the youngest in the state's history and the youngest in the nation at that time.

According to Cleo, he was *at-risk*, *disadvantaged*, and *underprivileged*—three terms he's fighting to get rid of as a member of Congress. He states, "When we stigmatize children because of their circumstances, we mess with their self-esteem. Here I was making *A's* and *B's* in classes and still classified as *at-risk*. Mom said to me, 'They are talking about your income, but you can't let that determine your outcome. Your mind is not disadvantaged. Your mind is not at-risk and your mind is not underprivileged.' " We must never forget that within every child is the desire and full capacity to learn.

We should all agonize over the damage
that society does to children living in poor
neighborhoods, but also over the enormous
damage that we do ourselves as a society
when we deny ourselves the gifts that
these children can give us.

— Jonathan Kozol

Chapter 1

Philosophy and Background of *Inspired to Learn*

Congratulations to Salisbury Middle
School teachers, support staff, parents, and
community. You've made believers out of
many who didn't believe we could do it. You
have truly inspired our children to learn and
you have armed them with the most powerful
weapon there is—KNOWLEDGE!

Among the first indicators of a positive
school climate and culture are the attitudes and
spirit of the teachers and staff in that school. I
was once told by a councilman on one of his
visits to our school [Salisbury Middle School],
"As I entered the building, I could literally
feel the synergy." He went on to comment
about the smiles and the engagement of the

adults and children he had observed during his visit to our school. Simply, everyone seemed to be happy and focused.

In most of today's schools, a very large percentage of students come from single-family homes. The realities and expectations of schools have changed dramatically over the past decade. Because of this, we must take a different approach to educating our children. This new approach should be based on the development of personal and appropriate relationships with staff, parents, the community, and students. For some, this is not a new approach, but simply an expansion of what they are currently doing. However, for others, this new model of education calls for the following:

- All students are to be valued and expected to learn to the best of their abilities.

- There is to be a stated mission, clearly-defined vision, and commitment of all to that mission/vision.

- Student-teacher relationships are to be long-term.

- Personal planning, goal setting, and career awareness are to be integrated into the curriculum.

- Curriculum and learning processes are to be adapted and modified to meet the learning needs of each student.

Drawing from my experiences both as a teacher and administrator, as we opened Salisbury Middle School in Salisbury, Maryland, in September 1999, I wanted to motivate, inspire, challenge, but more importantly, <u>lead</u> our faculty and staff. My experiences at Salisbury led me to write this book. I was provided with a clear pathway of understanding of what can truly happen in America's schools with the creation of a synergistic effort. When everyone is involved in the process of teaching and learning, failure is **not** an option.

As we attempt to reach and educate <u>all</u> of our children, one child at a time, it is my hope that the contents of *Inspired to Learn* will provide you with a vehicle to accomplish your specific goals in your school district and school community. Our children are depending on us more and more to capture, inspire, and restore their hope in the promise of a future that an education can lead them into. Over the years, I have become convinced that building positive, meaningful relationships with children is the answer.

I hope that you will enjoy the journey as you experience how young people respond to your sincere efforts in helping them to discover and to realize their dreams and aspirations.

Chapter 2

Laying the Foundation

Quality is never an accident. It is always
the result of sincere intention, diligent
effort, intelligent direction, and skillful
execution. It represents the wisest choice
of many alternatives.

There are many methods that can be used, and that are being used right this minute, to transform children at risk of failure into successful readers, writers, and learners. I wanted to learn all that I could to ensure opportunity and success for all of my students. Public education today is faced with many challenges: lack of funding, staffing, quality leadership and teachers, parental involvement, improper learning environments, and, an understanding of the cultures of today's youth, to name a few.

Educators seek answers and try many different approaches to resolve the same problems. The answers to the questions vary, depending on who answers them. I believe that the answers lie in our children and in our ability as educators, parents, and communities, to form positive relationships with them that will enable them to discover their own dreams and aspirations, the pursuit of which is the ultimate measure of the success of our efforts to educate them. In relationship with students, I always began by soliciting their cooperation. I understood that they were often living in situations as children that most adults would find deplorable. Yet, they were expected to come to school prepared and ready to learn. My approach as both a teacher and administrator was to develop them based on reciprocal respect. I respected them as a means of cultivating their respect toward me. It was important to also develop their trust. Establishing this type of relationship with students began to yield positive results. I became someone whom they wanted to see, to be around, to talk to, to listen to, and to connect with. Children who had caused others heartache were the ones I looked forward to being around each day.

"Just send him to Mr. Peters' class," rang out from my colleagues at C. Alton Lindsay Middle School. They were referring to students who were out of control in their classrooms. These students had already been sent to the office, suspended, conference with, and so on. Nothing seemed to work with them as they continued to repeat the same behavior. Many of the students who were sent to my classroom were children from broken homes with little hope. Lindsay was a large middle school with many children who fitted this description. Their chances were greatly reduced when they encountered adults who backed them into corners. Many youth today *expect* their interactions with adults in schools to be negative experiences. Unfortunately, it doesn't take long before their expectations are confirmed. Understanding this, I began my teaching career by spending quality time "capturing" my students. My personal belief is, "You can't teach a child until you've captured a child." It is impossible for the teaching and learning processes to take place before the capturing process has begun. Only then can any engaged learning take place.

Some of these students who had been chronically absent began to come to school on a more consistent basis. They also began to exhibit a more positive attitude toward school and about themselves. Trusting adults gradually became a possibility to many of them. Instead of continuing to impact our school negatively, they began to make a more positive impact. They didn't stop getting into trouble, but they were making progress. They began to see the purpose of school and how it fit into their lives. They now had a chance for a positive future.

Marvin came up to me on a bright, sunny Monday morning. You see, I had attended a teaching conference on the previous

Thursday and Friday. I said, "Good morning, Marvin." He responded, "Where were you last week?" "Last week?" "Thursday and Friday." First of all, it blew my mind that Marvin even knew that I was gone or that he cared for that matter. Secondly, it touched me at the deepest part of my soul that I'd finally reached him. He was "captured." We had formed a positive relationship that would prove to extend beyond the classroom or the school. When I speak of "capturing," I believe that it is the framework of success for the children in our public schools today. Marvin was definitely a child at risk. He was also a ring leader and constantly got into trouble in school and out. Nothing appeared to make him come around. Because I believed in my process, over time, he and I built a relationship that was based on reciprocal respect.

Marvin felt respected. Therefore, our interaction was always based on respect. Students need to know that the adults working with them, teaching them, coaching them, counseling them, mentoring them, truly care about them and their well being. As I walked into the clinic one day, a student told me that the reason he liked and respected me so much was that he knew I cared about him. I've been fortunate enough to work with some gifted individuals who share my belief on this issue. Over the years, they have confirmed the belief that our school's climate and culture is controlled by our internal belief systems. As we interact with our young people on a daily basis, we can't help but notice that most of them do not come to us ready and/or willing to learn. Many students have not had the appropriate amount of sleep, for whatever reason, nor do they have the right attitudes to enter a classroom to receive instruction from their respective teachers. For these reasons and due to many other issues our students are facing, e.g., abuse, (physical, sexual, and emotional), lack of proper nutrition, no one to help with homework or to share and communicate with, our schools must be prepared to compensate. I could never imagine having *control* of my classroom without having the *cooperation* and respect of my students. We were able to form such positive relationships that they did not ever want to see me in an uncomfortable situation.

Other teachers began sending students whom they were having trouble with to my classroom as a means of avoiding office referrals and, ultimately, suspensions. As I would awaken in the morning, I couldn't wait to get to school to interact, communicate, exchange information, capture and teach my wonderful students! Yes, wonderful! These young people have not had many successes in their lives. They have been forced to live with adult problems, issues, and circumstances. My interaction with them was one of the bright spots in their day. As time passed, we moved from the affective domain to the cognitive domain. Getting students to understand the importance of education became our focus. We had earned their trust and respect and could begin to make real changes happen for them and for those around them.

My relationship with my students deepened as we attempted to discover their dreams and aspirations. I would also share my own. This truly personalized the process for them. Getting them to think about the kind of life they wanted to live was certainly a starting point. Many students had no clue about the connection between education and success. They had no one to mirror this process for them in their homes. Their role models were neighborhood drug dealers or professional sports figures. Most of my students lived for the moment, the world of instant gratification. They found it very difficult to forecast their future.

Seeing young guys and girls making millions of dollars by rappin', many of my students dedicated their time, energies, and talents toward making rappin' their own realities. Unfortunately, as with other youngsters who aspire to become entertainers or professional athletes, the percentages of those who make it compared to those who don't is very low. This, however, does not impede the thought processes of those who want all of the material things they see in the music videos or elsewhere.

Talking to some of my students in the gym after school one day our conversation turned to very good athletes who never make it to the professional level. I shared with them the summary of my life's story. Basically, I grew up in a household of six children. When I began playing basketball, I was six years old. I practiced and played basketball every day until darkness fell. Year after year, I perfected my skills until I was considered one of the best in my state. Off to college I went on a full scholarship. There, I too dreamed of, some day, playing in the N.B.A.

My college career was filled with many highlights, the brightest being my college degree. At the completion of my four years, there was no N.B.A. contract. This was very devastating for me because I had spent my whole life preparing for something that was not going to happen. This was when my connection to life and the importance of education took shape. I was reminded by my mother, before she died, that I had earned a college degree that would afford me opportunities that people without a degree might not have. A teammate of mine from college was drafted into the N.B.A. He has done extremely well for himself and his family. All of our teammates are proud of his accomplishments and felt as if they were a part of it. At least one of us made it into the N.B.A.! However, I believe that I've "made it" also, but in another arena: Restoring hope to children who have lost hope has become my mission, my purpose in life.

Chapter 3

From a Student's Perspective

The one person in the school who has the most influence on the establishment of the environment that will produce achievement is the principal.

As a classroom teacher, I wanted each of my students to feel as if my teaching was directed toward them individually; as if each was the only one in the classroom. I was inspired by many of my students' efforts to identify and reach their unique potential. The eyes of my students mirrored the pain of their home lives, yet at the same time, I could also see their purity and hope for the future. I was determined, as many others, to make a positive difference in their lives. The most frustrating part of this equation was the fact that trust was not in any of my students' vocabulary. Completing the journey would take time.

Dr. Canady, our assistant superintendent, often visited our school. I was always impressed with his superior people skills. He remembered names and asked about the family and people's classes each time he approached them. He told me that I should begin to think about my future. For a brief moment, I thought that my job was in jeopardy. But instead, he was referring to my continuing education and becoming an administrator. I had not considered this option before that conversation. I thought I would teach forever. To this day, I attempt to identify leaders and I encourage others as he encouraged me. I enrolled in a graduate program as quickly as possible to begin learning all that I could about expanding my sphere of influence. I taught twenty to twenty-five different students in a class five times a day. While that was certainly a challenge, working with students and leading adults has presented challenges of a different kind.

My graduate program was an excellent one. It provided many practical experiences as well as solid research and leadership theories. The professors were impressive and many of them had been principals in the past. My professors knew that times had changed and that children, too, had changed. Some of the most interesting dialogues in my classes were about experiences during the course of a typical school day.

In graduate school, I met Dr. Ulysses Van Spiva, a professor whom I admired from the first night of class. There was something different about him; something that set him apart from many others I'd come across in my life. After he introduced himself, Dr. Spiva proceeded to share his expectations of us. He examined issues pertaining to education and how quickly things had changed. The more he talked, the more impressed I was. He appeared to be well versed in education and in life. He had a "Sidney Pointier" presence, yet he was humble. Dr. Spiva had received his Doctorate from Stanford University. He had worked odd jobs along the way. His eyes were always on the prize. He truly helped me understand the dynamics of life and the world. Far more than a teacher to me, he became a shaper of this part of my life as I searched for direction and purpose. He always encouraged me and he told me that I was going places fast. Since then, I seldom make career or life decisions without talking to my dear friend, "Vann."

Many graduate students worked all day and attended classes at night. Either my assignments kept me up until the early hours of the morning or I was up studying for an exam. I sometimes forgot that I had to get up to go to work the next morning. I always felt that I had a gift for working with children, particularly children "at risk." Whenever I would have a conversation with a young person or group of young people, they seemed to be captivated by whatever I was saying. They seemed to enjoy being around me. As I awaited the results of my comprehensive exam which determined whether I would receive my graduate degree or not, I became more and more excited about the possibility that I might be able to shine a light of hope on so many lost children.

I decided that my divine purpose in life was to motivate, capture, and inspire others to reach their fullest potential. If I worked with a teacher, I wanted to inspire that teacher to become the best he or she could become. I felt the same way about working with administrators, students, custodians, bus drivers, food service workers, secretaries and all other support staff. I began looking for jobs as a vice-principal. I found many open opportunities, particularly for African-American males. School systems all over the country were aggressively recruiting minority teachers as well. Finally, the long nights of studying, giving up weekends and time with my family, were about to pay off. Little did I know, I was about to embark on one of the most remarkable journeys of my life, one that would take me deep into the hearts and souls of children.

Choosing a school system to work in was one of my most difficult decisions. I had only worked in two schools: a private parochial school (right out of college), and a public middle school. At the time of my job search, my school district had no administrative openings. Therefore, my search took me outside of the school district where I had taught for eight years. Overall, it had been a good eight years. I had worked with some very good teachers and support staff. Our student body was as diverse as our professional staff.

Over the eight-year period, the difference between the two leaders of our school was that one was a leader (the principal) who would speak to you on Monday and may not speak to you again until Friday. (You also never quite knew what his vision or focus was.) The other was very personable and always attempted to make you feel that the school would not be the same without you. She was a worker, someone who helped with cafeteria duty, hall duty, and bus duty (things not usually associated with leaders). Her work ethic and approach caused many of her employees to go that "extra mile." We were always validated and shown appreciation for our work and efforts.

I reminded myself often that she was the kind of leader that I wanted to become. Before I completed my degree, I was nominated and selected to become a member of the board of directors for the Virginia Middle School Association. It was hard work, but an exciting learning experience. My exposure to other leaders and their leadership styles added immensely to my professional development. I began to pay closer attention to the commonalities of good leaders. Being a good leader is no more complicated than knowing who you are and what your job entails.

About fifteen years ago, the *Effective Schools Movement* gained recognition as a possible model for improving schools. Essentially, they looked at groups of high performing schools with the goal of identifying their similarities. In many ways, this effort was doing with schools what many in the business community were doing to meet the challenges of global competition. However, while a prescriptive approach might have worked with businesses, the same was not true with schools. Upon completing their study, the researchers found that much was shared by good schools and leaders. One of the components that they all had in common was "highly effective leadership."

Chapter 4

Shifting Paradigms: Moving On

Here's all that's certain about the future: It
holds profound and unpredictable change.

— Peter F. Drucker

School change is happening, but not on a
scale that meets the growing needs of our
student population.

— Bev Elzey, Counselor

In many ways, talking about leadership is
like talking about shooting a basketball or
hitting a golf ball. If Michael Jordan (possibly
the best basketball player of all time) or Tiger
Woods (by far the best golfer in the world)
had stopped by my neighborhood when I was
a kid and spent an hour talking to me about

how to shoot or hit, I doubt I would have been any better than I turned out to be. However, it is certainly possible that they would have inspired me to practice more and that the additional work would have made me better on the court or golf course. Many of the leaders and other educators whom I began meeting while I served as a board member of the Virginia Middle Schools Association inspired me to become the best leader that I could possibly become.

Fifteen to twenty years ago, principals went through the day making sure that they returned phone calls, opened and responded to mail, talked with teachers, and made sure that the buses arrived and departed on schedule. So much has changed in our homes and schools across America that today, this management style would fall short of leadership. Our parents, community, students, and teachers require us to be visionary in our approach. We have to be motivators, bringing the best out of our employees and moving them in the direction that will ultimately impact our schools in the best possible manner. Leaders today are also required to be visible. As we attempt to "capture" our staff and students, we have to be both accessible and available. Often, when we are called upon, it is because someone wants to be heard. Listening to their concerns will usually take care of the issue(s) they bring to us. This is very important because the person who comes to us feels a sense of value and is more likely to become an ambassador for the school.

The visibility of principals is the key to many issues schools encounter on a daily basis. Because the demands upon the "new leader" are ever changing, closer attention is paid to the vice principal. Vice principals must function at a higher level as school managers. Let's take a look at what this entails. The columns on the following page profile the principal and vice principal functions.

Principal	Vice Principal
As	*As*
Visionary	Manager
Instructional Leader	Sub-finder
Public Relations Marketer	Observer
Business-Partner's Coordinator	Facilities
Teacher/Student Advocate	Transportation
Visible/Accessible	Discipline

As a principal, and now director of different educational ventures, I was probably most effective as a leader during my very first year. At that time, failure was not an option. Things had to go well and when they didn't, I would establish the type of relationship with my staff so that they would rally around me to make things happen. At its best, this illustrates a positive school or organizational climate, driven by underlying belief systems. Our belief system was, "Everyone is on the same team." School climate and culture largely depends on the ability of the principal and the vice principals functioning at a high performance level. One of the major challenges we face is dealing reasonably with the culture of families, children, and today's society. Homes and children have changed dramatically and schools and school boards have been slow to make the necessary changes and to adjust to the problems associated with those changes.

Dr. Gene Carter, the *Executive Director of the Association for Supervision and Curriculum Development (A.S.C.D.)*, was the superintendent who hired me in Norfolk, Virginia. I will always remember my interview with him. He had such a presence about him and for the first time in my life, I felt nervous about talking to someone. When I left Dr. Carter's conference room that afternoon I was convinced that he was surely someone to be admired both personally and professionally. Dr. Carter gave me the opportunity to become a vice principal in a school with professional educators who had what it took to make a difference. The time I spent at Northside Middle School helped to lay the foundation that shaped my belief systems and values about leadership and people.

At Northside, Dr. Robert "Bob" Hahne was the principal and Mrs. Brenda King was the other vice principal. I learned many valuable lessons from both of them. The most important was the importance of forming personal relationships with students and staff. "Bob," as we called him, believed in Ron Edmonds' philosophy and ran his school in a style that echoed Edmonds and Tom Peters. Ron Edmonds highlighted seven correlations of effective schools:

- *Clear and Focused Mission*
- *Safe, Orderly, and Caring Environment*
- *Opportunity to Learn*
- *High Expectations for Success*
- *Frequent Monitoring of Student Progress*
- *Instructional Leadership*
- *Home–School–Community Relations*

Within the structure of our school, we all knew our roles and performed them well. We were also very well aware that if we didn't do our jobs well, our primary customers, the students, would suffer.

Bob ran what Larry Lazote would define as a "loosely coupled organization," where everyone operated within a specific framework. Everyone knew their general and specific job functions and knew them well. Within this framework, when decisions needed to be made, each employee was empowered to make them. I cannot remember anyone ever being afraid of failing or making a wrong decision. My role here was to ensure that my "customers" were always taken care of. Who were my customers? My teachers/support staff, students, parents, and my boss. My job was to handle as much as possible without going to him. In this way, he would be able to lead and not have to manage. At Northside, as an assistant principal, Bob always encouraged and empowered me to make decisions. When things went well, he would tell me, "Good job." When things went badly he would ask, "If you had it to do over again, what would you do?" Working in this type of environment helped to shape some of my intrinsic views about leadership. My administrative experiences have encompassed a broad spectrum of leadership styles, from the autocratic to the empowering. From these two experiences, I formed some definite feelings about how I would operate as a leader. I knew that I would not be autocratic, because too many people would be waiting for the things that I initiated to fail. It just wasn't in me to operate in that manner. As a basketball player, I had played the position of point guard. John Bryant, the C.E.O. of a very successful company used most of the same mental skills and talents he had used on the football field. The preparation, discipline, focus, skills, and determination were the same. The only difference was that he was in a board room.

While at Northside, the school district sent me to be assessed as a leader. I was administered a series of exercises for three days that depicted the real life, day-to-day experiences that leaders face. The basis for determination was the National Association of Secondary School Principal's (N.A.S.S.P.) assessment instrument which rated candidates' abilities in several areas, including: decisiveness, range of interests, stress tolerance, oral and written communication skills, problem analysis, and leadership. Coming out of this experience, many of us felt overwhelmed and knew that we all had our work cut out for us in the real world. When I received my report in a meeting with one of the four assessors, I was quite pleased that my results were higher than anyone else's in the history of this regional assessment center. The assessment validated the natural skills and talents I believed that I possessed. Knowing this bolstered my confidence about being able to do the job and do it well!

When I think of Northside, the word "synergy" comes to mind. As we entered the second semester, our interest peaked around qualifying for "Blue-Ribbon" status. This award is given to 20 percent of all of the schools in America. The teachers in our building represented some of the best in the country and they knew it. They had the ability to "capture" students to the degree that these students wanted to be taught. The students wanted to absorb everything that these teachers put out to them as though they were sponges. We had the usual fights and behavioral problems just like every other inner-city school in America. The difference was in the manner that we chose to deal with the issues. We had the ability and the foresight to turn negative into positive. That is what sets excellent schools apart from good schools. We were an excellent school! Our administrators were excellent, our teachers and support staff were excellent, our students were excellent, and our parents supported our vision and mission. When the visiting team from Washington, D.C., came to observe for themselves what had been written in our Blue-Ribbon application, they saw a very natural process. The positive energy that they felt as they walked the halls and entered classrooms was one of the determining factors in their decision to confer upon us the distinction of *National Blue-Ribbon School.*

The initiatives described on the following pages represent the smorgasbord of ideas and processes that were implemented at Northside Middle School that led to the many awards and distinctions bestowed upon our school. Unlike many documents that propagate the latest trends in research and development, our initiatives defined what was effective for all students at the delivery level. Beyond outcome-based performance, quality is measured by an underlying spirit of cooperation, collaboration, caring, and trust. Our work at Northside clearly exemplified teacher commitment, not only to basic cognition, but to the developmental interest of every child. Missing from most research related to organizational or instructional improvement are the contextual factors that promote or impede successful implementation.

As a *National Blue Ribbon* and a *Virginia Vanguard School,* we were given the unique opportunity to test reliable research, as well as site-based initiatives in a constructive fashion. The following is an abbreviated edition of the "good stuff" we used and that I continue to use wherever I am called. These processes can be especially useful for educational practitioners, not for university researchers.

<u>School Demographics</u>

Number of students enrolled at each grade level:

6th - 452

7th - 416

8th - <u>374</u>

1,242 - Total Students

Racial/Ethnic composition:

0.8% American Indian or Native Alaskan

3.9% Asian or Pacific Islander

46.0% Black, not Hispanic origin

2.3% Hispanic

<u>47.0%</u> White, not Hispanic origin

100.0% TOTAL

Cooperation among the school, parents, and the community at-large fostered relationships which contributed to the nurturing environment at Northside. In every sense of the word, Northside Middle was a "family" school. Located in a predominately working, middle-class neighborhood, forty percent of our students walked to school with the remainder being bused in from military and public housing. This provided a diverse cultural and socio-economic population.

New Generation of American Schools

According to the U.S. Department of Education's report, *AMERICA 2000: An Education Strategy,* schools must:

- look beyond the confines of their immediate surroundings;

- prepare themselves to be more accountable to their constituents; and,

- ensure that results are centered around measurable student outcomes.

Northside exemplified the essence of this philosophy. The school restructured the organization of management for the closer monitoring of students. The strategic planning process was a collective vision of the entire staff, which fostered greater communication among administration, faculty, parents, and the community to meet the needs of our students. Further, shared decision-making always helps to promote "ownership." Devotion and dedication to all was the force behind the vision which drove us toward excellence. Students always knew that someone cared about them. School became a home away from home for all of the members of our "family." Our commitment to students resulted in significant gains in student performance and quality instruction.

Beyond The Expected

Innovative uses of time included:

- Extension of the regular school day to provide additional opportunities for students to experience success.

- Saturday School as an alternative to out-of-school suspensions.

- Extended-day tutoring.

- Block scheduling to allow flexibility for interdisciplinary instruction.

- Satellite classrooms to perpetuate and reinforce the teaching and learning processes from a global perspective.

Administrative Leadership

Principals should always encourage teachers and staff to take a proactive role in the decision-making process. In the schools I've been a part of, I have always had an open-door policy to encourage the sharing of concerns or ideas. Input is solicited throughout the staff and communities. The contributions of others can have a direct effect on school policies and procedures. Students and faculty members should be encouraged to pursue personal and professional growth. The principal should provide support, including financial support, for all pursuits that will drive the school toward pursuing its mission and achieving its vision. The collegial spirit of Northside was nurtured through informal gatherings. Students, parents, and faculty members got together several times a month to meet, greet, discuss, and share. This provided a non-threatening environment for pulling people together for the greater good of our school.

Teacher Involvement

Northside was subdivided by grade level, with an administrator responsible for each level. Cluster or team teachers met regularly with their grade level administrators, and periodically with the principal, allowing their input in the decision-making process. Further opportunities were made available through department chairpersons. Committees were designed based on the eight correlations of effective schools. These committees were school improvement teams which helped to formulate the school's strategic plan of action. The school improvement committee, consisting of the principal, assistant principal, dean of students, three faculty-selected teachers/support staff, and the PTA president, regularly reviewed school programs and policies to analyze and resolve school problems effectively. There was also an instructional council composed of the principal and department chairpersons which made curricular and instructional recommendations and decisions.

Planning

Northside's interdisciplinary clustering consisted of four core subject area teachers. In most cases, additional faculty members from physical education and the electives were also a part of the cluster team. The physical education and elective departments also participated in their own cluster called the "Northside Stars." Each cluster member shared a common planning time wherein the preparation of interdisciplinary units, parent-teacher conferences, the evaluation of student progress, and the formulation of innovative programs and projects were discussed. The implementation of recommendations from clusters extended into the various existing committees. Teachers also served on committees stemming from central administration.

Teacher Support Systems

To ensure the success of beginning teachers, they were automatically assigned a veteran buddy teacher or mentor. The teacher-mentor relationships provided support and guidance for a "rookie" throughout the year. New teachers in this program participated in mentor/mentee observation/feedback sessions, workshops, group discussions, and other selected activities with the hope of providing opportunities for strengthening the foundation of teaching and learning.

Recognition

A positive school climate helps to support and to encourage staff by extending their skills and levels of expertise through extrinsic and intrinsic rewards. Selection as a mentor in the "Teacher-Mentor Program" was an initial step. A "Teacher of the Year" was also selected to represent the school at the district level, and if selected, in the state or national competitions. Further opportunities for recognition were made through the principal's staff recognition program called the "Apple Awards." There were eleven categories of entry and an overall award to the teacher/staff member who had contributed the most toward the greater good of the school.

Job Satisfaction

We recognized that the schedule was a powerful tool. The establishment of a Scheduling Committee enabled teachers to have direct input regarding the construction and/or modification of the schedule. Within the clusters, teachers had the autonomy and flexibility to make scheduling changes for their students.

Staff Development

The School Improvement Committee, at the close of each school year, established the areas of emphasis for the upcoming school year. The principal then outlined a budget, reflecting the goals set forth by this body. Further contact was made with Staff Development to inquire about the opportunities already available through their department. Conferences, workshops, seminars, and in-service activities were established throughout the year, including during the summer, to support the overall mission of the school. Teachers were asked to share acquired knowledge in faculty meetings, cluster meetings, and formal in-service activities.

Curriculum and Instruction

The mission of our school system was "teaching for learning." At Northside, we believed that "all teachers can teach and all students can learn." Therefore, we adopted the theme "Switch On The Dream" to reflect this attitude. We provided a solid transition for the students from elementary to middle to high school. Sixth graders had longer periods of interaction with one teacher, and were housed in one part of the school building to foster confidence in a new environment. In the seventh grade, there was an increased focus on emotional and sociological development, relative to the adjustment to the middle school philosophy. The emphasis in the eighth grade was on meeting the challenges of high school. This elaborate progression provided students with the awareness of coursework responsibilities and the attendant privileges of maturation levels.

The heterogeneous grouping of students allowed for cooperative and collaborative instruction. Peer tutoring, cooperative learning, and individualized learning environments addressed the varying needs of all students. Those students who had been classified as "gifted" could not be infused into all clusters by academic areas. However, opportunities were made available for students to move into and out of these sections as needed.

Whenever I run into one of our former Northside students they always comment on their "Northside days." Middle school provided them with experiences that will last a lifetime. We had armed our students with the most powerful weapon there is—Knowledge. Many generational patterns were broken through our conscious efforts to cultivate our school's climate and culture. However, we were able to help our students to understand the connection between continuing their education to live a better life. Many of our students entered college and were the first members in their families to do so.

Very Special Education

Since the diverse student population at Northside required teachers to assess learning styles and personality types in the teaching process through varied instructional programs, "Switch(ing) on the Dream" for all students was increasingly important. "Believe-Achieve-Succeed," is the underlying premise from which our special education program operated. All students under the umbrella of special education were expected to experience success and were a part of an interdisciplinary team. Students who were capable of remaining in the mainstream were in classes where the student-teacher ratio did not exceed 20:1 in a "co-teaching" environment.

Remediation for these students took place in the regular classroom with a special education teacher, during a scheduled resource class or in specially-designed developmental courses such as "Power Math." Students requiring remediation in reading were identified through functional reading scores and teacher observation. To help self-contained and learning-disabled students who had not learned to read under traditional basal reading programs, the Standard Reading Assessment (SRA) Corrective Reading Program was established. The lessons were scripted using carefully sequenced tasks offering the necessary structure of skills. Positive reinforcement was also a fundamental component of this process.

Assessment

An annual School Improvement Plan, which included goals and specific objectives to be achieved, was developed by the School Improvement Team. Strategies and activities were listed and assigned to individuals with a targeted completion date. In addition to standardized test scores our school system provided each school with monitor and mastery test information which was desegregated to analyze varying socio-economic group performance. Department chairpersons and administrators worked with teachers to use this information to monitor individual student performance and to strengthen the instructional process.

Preparing For the Future

The common objectives of the different schools and school districts where I have worked are: to prepare our students for living in a society that is globally competitive; to foster positive attitudes regarding different cultures; to reinforce a process-oriented approach to science, math, writing, and utilizing increasingly sophisticated technology. Since the future will demand advanced technical, mathematical, and problem-solving skills, the following goals should be priorities for all students:

- Exposure to cultures other than their own so that they will gain respect for those who are different.

- Integrating special education students into regular classrooms.

- Enrolling students in "Careers and You," which explores careers in the fifteen job clusters identified by the United States Department of Labor.

- Exposure to the global events taking place daily.

- Offering at least three foreign languages in the curriculum, as well as other exploratory classes.

Response to Research

In response to current research and development initiatives, the school and community must react by showing a commitment to the environmental and instructional factors that support constructive teaching and learning. Having withstood various tests of empirical verification, the following strategies should be employed:

- Institute continuous, progressive learning.

- Pay attention to higher order skills.

- Re-define courses and credits in modern terms.

- Promote site-based management for more effective planning and implementation.

- Utilize outcome-based, value-added education.

- Adopt the role of teacher and principal as coach.

- Establish extended-day and extended-week instruction.

- Encourage risk takers.

- Increase cross teaching, subject teaming, and interdisciplinary training.

- Train more creative, caring, and hard-working teachers and administrators.

- Develop a proper climate for change.

- Make a strong effort to understand students' social environments.

- Identify what is really important to teach and concentrate on those skills.

- Teach administrators conflict management.

- Promote shared decision-making.

- Implement block scheduling.

- Work at integrating technology, i.e., computers, televisions, interactive video-instruction.

- Involve parents and community members, meaningfully, in the life of the school.

Secrets to Success

The following conditions can contribute to the success of any school's team of educators:

- Implementation of an effective School Improvement Team.

- Empowerment of teachers through decentralization of decision making within the school.

- Lateral management philosophy, fostering a "loosely coupled" organizational structure.

- Specialized programs/processes (e.g., The Gentlemen's and Ladies' Clubs).

- Compensatory reading programs.

Challenges For the Future

Over the next five years, schools will face the following educational challenges:

- Providing a safe and secure environment conducive to learning.

- Providing students with a solid foundation in core subject areas according to the expressed goals of national and state initiatives to ensure success in high school and in higher education endeavors.

- Increasing the number of lower socio-economic students taking advanced courses.

- Preparing staff members for future roles as administrative leaders.

- Preparing students to make informed choices academically, vocationally, and socially.

- Preparing students to be successful on high school assessment exams.

To ensure our readiness for being responsive to changing student needs, the role of staff development is crucial. Through individual and collective efforts, we must remain on the leading edge of issues, trends, and strategies for effective teaching.

Chapter 5

Survival Skills for the New Principal

My goals as a beginning principal were to be a visionary, to be the instructional leader of our school, and to maintain a positive school climate.

Much of what is done on a daily basis to ensure success for our children is not learned in a graduate program.

— Cathy J. Townsend
Middle School Principal, Maryland

I will never forget the evening that I received a phone call from my Assistant Superintendent informing me that I was being assigned to the principalship of the largest middle school in Norfolk, Virginia. I was about to complete my first year as assistant principal when the news came. Quite frankly, I was enjoying everything about our school and the journey that we were making toward fulfilling our vision. We had just been honored with the distinction of *National Blue Ribbon School* and felt that we could really build on this to inspire even more of our children to believe in their dreams. As I anticipated my new assignment I couldn't help but focus on the people who had influenced my ideas and philosophies. I would now carry their inspiration with me as I chartered new waters.

After accepting the new position I did some research on the school that I would be leading in a different direction. What I found was astounding! The school was one year old. The physical structure and design were beautiful. The problem was that in the first year the school had experienced a shooting at the buses and four students had been injured. Along with low test scores, low student and staff morale, this shooting represented the impetus for change. The school was 65 percent African-American, 30 percent white, and 5 percent Asian. Many of the parents did not feel safe about their children being in this school. Most of the teachers there were good teachers, but morale was low for many reasons. Our work was cut out for us!

We (please notice that I said "we") began by assessing the damage, reviewing test scores, listening to parents, community members, patrons, students, teachers, custodians, bus drivers, and anyone else who had a connection to the school. We didn't try to make excuses or cover up anything. We were attempting to put the pieces together that would restore the trust of our customers. Yes, our customers! Our primary customers were the students, then the parents, community, and taxpayers. As the summer approached I was far too busy to get nervous about anything. We moved from one segment of planning to another. As I worked with my administrative team, we decided not to change much about the operational structure in the first year. We would observe what worked and why; what didn't work and why.

What we would change was the belief system or culture in which we would operate. We anticipated that a high level of respect would be given to our students, teachers, support staff, parents, and community. We operated under the premise that respect was to be reciprocated at all levels. Many wonderful things could take place with this type of culture in place. Teachers would want to come to work because they felt that they were a part of the decision-making process. They felt ownership and wanted to do their part to the best of their abilities.

We listened to parents so much that they became willing to listen to what we had to say. We made only one promise: that we would treat their child(ren) the way we would want our own biological children to be treated. This got their attention because what better service could you receive? As we moved forward with our planning that summer I set a goal to meet personally with all of my teachers. Appointments were scheduled for each teacher. In these meetings, I heard their frustrations and expectations of me as their leader. I credit these meetings as the one thing that began to establish our culture. I knew what they expected from me and they knew what I expected from them. We all had the same basic goals in mind: to provide the highest degree of quality to our students and to have fun doing it.

As the school year began, our idealistic and optimistic attitudes would help to get us through some bumpy times, some fights, and finally to discussions pertaining to instruction and assessment. We were making progress toward our mission/vision. We got through our first year on a high feeling. There wasn't anything that we couldn't do with or for our students. I remember handwriting thank you notes to my teachers on Sunday afternoons at the office and how much they appreciated those notes. (By the way, this doesn't cost anything.) We would go into our next year with a renewed focus on quality instruction and specialized programs for the children whom we felt were "at risk."

During the course of my first year as a principal, having served as a vice principal for only one year, I knew that I needed to surround myself with the very best faculty and support staff I could find. While my goals were clear, realistically, I knew that many obstacles could come my way and prevent me from serving in the sole capacity of instructional leader. I also spent quality time counseling those who were unable to help their students to flourish. This was accomplished by working closely with them over a period of time. After all, good teaching is hard and demanding work. Observing the culture of my new school from a community, staff and student perspective, I realized that we had a long way to go. When staff morale is low, it affects every area of operation, especially the instructional program.

Assuming that good decisions have been made regarding hiring most teachers and motivating those who are not effective, principals must also find ways to help teachers to continue growing. They have control in the classroom, i.e., they are empowered to take care of problems in their own rooms and to use principals as advisors, not punishers. To illustrate this point, I share a true story. About six months into my first year of teaching, a student in one of my classes was having a rough day. It appeared that he was not happy about being in school or around me. One day I was pushing him to work harder and to come into my classroom better prepared when he said, "I hate you. Get the hell out of my face." To say the least, I was shocked. I had not learned how to handle a situation like this in my master's program. Since no one had told me what to do I handled it on instinct. The critical and determining moments with students occur in the beginning. We very seldom get to take back words or actions that hurt or offend. Realizing this to be one of those determining moments, I <u>asked</u> the young man to step out into the hallway so that I could have a word with him. Instead of embarrassing him by writing him up in front of his peers and sending him to the office for a suspension, I chose to allow him to save face and I used this opportunity to establish a different type of relationship with him.

As we entered the hallway, instead of attacking him, I shared with him that I felt hurt by his outburst in the classroom. I asked him if there was anything I could do to help him to deal with whatever was bothering him. My approach startled him as he anticipated a verbal lashing, which he was accustomed to receiving from the adults in his life. I shared with him that I would not be writing an office referral for him that afternoon, but that if this pattern of behavior continued, he would leave me no other alternative. Further, I made it clear that this was my choice, because I felt that there were other issues that had caused the behavior. As we both began our return to the classroom he looked at me with admiration. He was both impressed with the gentle manner of his teacher and relieved that his behavior did not cause him to get suspended this time.

The next day, this student asked if he

could speak with me after class. He told me, "Mr. Peters, I want to apologize for my behavior yesterday." I accepted his apology and we moved on. This student became one of my best students during that school year. Our relationship would have been totally different based on the handling of a single experience. He became one of the students who never wanted to see me in an uncomfortable situation. Teachers also must view their vice principals and principals as facilitators, not punishers. When they take effective classroom management practices to heart, it clears the way for enhanced student learning.

Classes, workshops, and publications address the characteristics and behaviors of exemplary teachers, but few explain the role of the exemplary leader. Let's take a look at the exemplary principal.

The Exemplary Principal as:

- A person
- A visionary
- An instructional leader
- A problem solver
- A manager
- A school-community facilitator

The Principal as a Person:

- Inspires confidence and inspires others
- Uses effective verbal, written, listening, and interpersonal skills
- Generates enthusiasm
- Possesses high energy and a relentlessly positive nature
- Has a sense of humor

The Principal as a Visionary:

- Has a clear vision of what a great school is

- Possesses the will and the desire to go after that vision

- Leads the way in developing the operational strategies needed to fulfill the vision

- Can explain his or her philosophy and vision to others

- Has the ability to develop, to communicate, and to persuade others to support a vision of education for young adolescents, which becomes the driving force for the school

- Is committed to developing a mentally responsive and developmentally appropriate educational environment

- Sets high academic goals for all students

The Principal as an Instructional Leader:

- Is knowledgeable about the curriculum, programs, and practices

- Understands the unique nature of the "new learner"

- Has a deep understanding of curriculum instruction and the skills necessary for effective school leadership

- Engages the faculty in continuous improvement

- Is knowledgeable about curriculum and teaching methods

- Promotes continuous staff development through personal example and by his or her actions (attending and sending teachers to workshops and conferences)

The Principal as a Leader of an Educational Organization:

- Exhibits leadership
- Inspires teachers to exceed expectations
- Supports teachers
- Is accessible to staff
- Remains highly visible to faculty and students in the hallways, classrooms, in the lunchroom, on the television, all over the campus and considers his or her role as being more than the chief disciplinarian

The Principal as a Manager:

- Is knowledgeable and effectively plans a budget
- Can identify, hire, motivate, and evaluate other staff members
- Gets the job done

The Principal as a School-Community Facilitator:

- Inspires parents, faculty, community, and students to "buy into" the belief that the school belongs to everyone

- Shows sensitivity to the needs of a racially and culturally diverse school and community population

- Deals effectively with parents who may challenge the school's mission to serve all students well

As a new principal, I never expected to have to confront so many situations with which I was not familiar. The importance of surrounding yourself with a quality staff was the lesson I learned. The energy I exerted as a "rookie" was to create synergy among all staff and students by providing as much assistance as possible to bring them into our vision. Many of our students depended on us to be there for them on a daily basis. For this to occur, our focus and attitudes were of the utmost importance. Building positive relationships with staff, students, and parents would require me, as the leader, to "seek first to understand, then be understood" (Stephen Covey).

On Sunday afternoons, I would hand-write notes to my teachers and support staff members affirming the work that they were doing.

Dear Mr/Mrs. Teacher,

Just a quick note to thank you for helping Ryan by offering to tutor him after school. Teachers like you truly make a difference. Our school would not be the same without you.

Sincerely,
Stephen G. Peters
Principal

Informal notes like this made a difference with our staff. They felt validated and appreciated. On days when they had a headache and might have stayed at home, they instead made the decision to come to work. Many of the indicators of effective schools began simply by changing the way people dealt with each other. Building positive relationships would continue to be our focus as we restored hope in each other and, more importantly, in our children. There was ownership of our vision and mission because we were all involved in the decision-making process. We had created a synergistic effort toward becoming the kind of school we had dreamed of becoming. We were now on our way!

Before moving on, I'd like to share some of the hurdles that new principals consistently face as they attempt to become change agents and advocates for students.

The Principal's Facts of Life

The ghosts of the past still rule the school.

Although invisible, the image of the last principal haunts the current leader. Even though school faculty and staff noted the principal's shortcomings while he/she led the school, they endow him/her with saintly virtues after he/she is gone. The new leader must acknowledge and respect the ghosts of his or her predecessor.

The culture of the school is deeply embedded in the practices and expectations of each staff member.

Teachers who say, "We've always done it that way," are not necessarily afraid of change. Long-standing leadership offers consistency that gives meaning and security to teachers' professional lives. New principals need to learn and respect their school's culture.

Stephen G. Peters

Once you walk across the principal's threshold, all relationships change.

The new principal may look the same, hold identical beliefs, and express himself or herself as clearly as when he or she was a teacher. Teachers, parents, and children, however, perceive the principal as the ultimate seat of wisdom and authority in the school. Even leaders who are promoted from within a school find their former colleagues hushing the conversation when their new "boss" walks into the room.

The principalship is a very lonely world.

Although surrounded by people all day, the principal soon learns that it is lonely at the top.

The principal rarely wins a popularity contest.

The decisions that principals have to make almost always displease someone. Parents are often concerned about the welfare of their children. A teacher may not realize that the broken air conditioner in her homeroom is not at the top of the principal's priority list.

The work never gets done.

New principals may work late into the evening and on weekends to finish paperwork. By Monday afternoon the paperwork has piled up again. All school leaders experience this phenomenon, but new principals may feel overwhelmed.

Some Practical Tips

Take heart. Most principals really do survive the first year. Veteran principals become accustomed to the workload and the loneliness, and they slowly become a part of the culture, even as they influence it. Principals learn that change comes slowly through strong relationships with staff, parents, and students. As a result, remarkable leaders can develop in today's schools. New principals might avoid some common pitfalls by reflecting on the following ideas:

1. Respect the past with its heroes, heroines, icons, and rituals. The

school secretary is often the custodian of the culture and the heartbeat of its informal communication system. If you want to know about the school's culture or history, ask the secretary. Always treat the secretary and others as professionals.

2. Meet each teacher and department chairperson. New leaders should constantly ask their staff and faculty two questions:

   What do you truly value and want to retain about the school at all costs?

   What needs to be discarded from the school?

   These questions, phrased effectively, will elicit some valuable advice.

3. Locate the power. Bring those with power; teachers, parents, and even the individuals who applied for your job into the loop of your influence. Seek their advice. It's better to keep powerful

people on your team rather than have them plot your downfall.

4. Keep the central office informed. The superintendent and central office staff can be your allies or your critics.

5. Take care of yourself physically, emotionally, professionally, and spiritually. Make sure to make time to exercise and stay involved in activities you enjoy.

6. Pick your battles. Not every issue needs to be addressed. Write your personal mission statement and clearly define, in your own mind, what you stand for.

7. Continue to learn. No principal ever consults a college textbook for the answer to a problem. Attend professional conferences and continue to read.

Schools need principals who understand that schools are human endeavors—continually evolving dynamic organisms. Despite the demands of the principalship and the challenges of the first year, an effective leader has the power to help teachers and students learn and grow in profound ways.

Stay true to your mission and stay focused on your vision. As Mychal Wynn so eloquently articulates in his book, *Increasing Student Achievement: Volume I Vision*, "Every decision must ultimately be measured by 'What's in the best interests of students?' "

Chapter 6

The Importance
of Vision

We all have dreams of shaping a project in
our vision along with a high-energy,
productive team. The vision at Salisbury
Middle School was to create synergy and to
capture as many young people as we could.

In a period of rapid structural change, the
only organizations that survive are the
change leaders.

— Brian Curtis, Co-Facilitator
The Gentlemen's Club, Maryland

Research on successful school reform
reveals that several years are required, usually
a minimum of three, and that teachers and
their instructional practices should be at the
core of reform, (Fulham & Hargreaves, 1992;

Goodland, 1990; Sarason, 1993). The failure of school reform is often attributed to the lack of change in the basic structure, policies, and instructional practices of the school or systems, because teachers are not involved in the process. In many school systems teachers are on the periphery of change and are seen in very traditional ways. They are viewed as having command of their isolated classrooms, but not as leaders in their respective schools. However, both practice and research indicate that when seeking a different outcome for student performance or a higher level of achievement, involving teachers in the process is crucial to the endeavor (Boyer, 1995; Fulham, 1993; Sarason, 1996; Darling-Hammond, 1995).

The more we understand how change happens the more we can anticipate the journey, enabling us to better manage our responses to it. Knowing ourselves helps us to separate our personal reactions to change from our professional reactions to the process of change itself. Being sensitive to what is happening in the world around us and how events affect us personally and at school is very important in understanding our response to change. As we read the newspaper and watch the news each day many of the stories echo the halls of our school buildings pertinent to the futures of our children. We could probably have some of our teachers predict who would most likely follow in the footsteps of the people in the news whom we read and hear about each day. For many children, we are not only their hope, we are their *last* hope. In the framework of the big picture we need to prioritize our goals and make restoring hope to our children the most important thing we can possibly do as they enter our school buildings every day.

Schools have been transformed into buildings where administrators and teachers are attempting to provide environments that are conducive to learning. The processes of teaching and learning have taken a back seat to that of providing a safe environment for students. The challenge we face is to find ways, in spite of what's happening in society and in homes, to provide a quality education for all of our children. The climates and cultures of our schools are ultimately the keys to the success of our schools. Everything we do, on a daily basis, should be tied to the question, *Is this in the best interest of children?* When we put children first, positive things begin to happen in our schools. Our children have a keen sense of how much we care about them, as well as our interest in their futures. Once established, our relationships with the children in our schools will determine many of the outcomes of our schools. As educators, we tend to believe that we are the ones who have the answers. I have talked with children for more than seventeen years and I believe children have always steered *me* in the right direction. Most of the time children are honest about the issues we face in our schools. They also ask insightful questions and should always be provided with a forum for asking and receiving answers to their questions. When students are included in the process we create a new level of synergy. My experience has taught me that the potential for growth in our schools today rests with how deeply we establish relationships with the children whom we serve. There were 900 students and 100 adults in our building. The students could have taken over any time they wanted to. *Who was really in charge? What stopped the students from taking over?* I say, it was the respect and ownership that had been so carefully established.

Respect is reciprocal; it is given and received. If students feel that they are treated like human beings, people with dignity, the more they are willing to "buy-in." Isn't this the piece we're missing? Students want structure and direction. It's when they don't receive it, and we, as adults, still attempt to hold them accountable. For every inconsistent rule that one teacher follows and another doesn't, trouble begins or wounds already present become deeper. As we deal with one behavioral problem after another, less and less teaching and learning is taking place. Through researching the process of discipline in our school we discovered that we needed to move in a direction that would afford us an opportunity to spend less time with discipline and more time dealing with instructional issues and practices.

The first step was to gain "buy-in" and to come to a consensus that we really needed help from each other to make this work. It was easy because our entire staff wanted to be able to provide the very best service to our children. So, we committed to a series of classes on cooperative discipline that would last for five consecutive weeks for three hours a session. This process would begin to bring us together in ways that we knew would make the difference day to day. We had to establish a procedure for our building that would require all of us to do our parts, knowing if we didn't it would have a negative impact on the whole organization. We would be as strong as our weakest link. As the leader of our school, I began to see teachers and support staff going the extra mile to make our school a better place for our students and us.

Staffing our schools with the best administrators, teachers, and support staff is the most important thing to do for laying a foundation of quality in our schools. At my former middle school I was blessed and fortunate enough to interview and hire 70 percent of my staff. As my school was being constructed, I had one year to order furniture, meet with curriculum directors, facility engineers, and human resource personnel to prepare for a very important future in the history of our school system.

The most important piece was to begin the type of staffing we had decided upon. First, we moved the sixth grade students and teachers to the middle school. Many of them wanted to move, but some wanted to stay at the elementary level. Another major issue was that we had three other middle schools to be staffed. The new school where I would serve as principal was state-of-the-art, with one computer for every two students—certainly an attraction to those who were interested in having the latest in technology and a new start. Many of the teachers and others wanted to work with a leader whom they perceived to be a visionary and a motivator. I believed that our success would be directly related to making a difference regardless of where our children lived, something that others could not accomplish with their children. When things did not go well, we took it personally and felt there was more that we could and should do for our children and our school.

After determining how many and who would be moving from elementary to middle school, and determining who would go where, we had to deal with transfer requests from teachers and how many vacant positions needed to be filled with new employees. During the course of my year of overseeing the construction of the building, I met numerous district teachers and staff members. I started a "Book Club," which was really a study circle group that met once a month to discuss our book of choice. We first selected and discussed Stephen Covey's, *Seven Habits of Highly Effective People.* The group was open to any of our district teachers/staff. Through this group I got to know some of our district's top teachers, and they also, got to know me as a person along with my views on leadership. This experience served as the catalyst for me to hire the very best in our field.

As we began the process of interviewing many of us realized how critical each position truly was, as well as how it was tied to the big picture: a school that would provide high-quality service to children every day, that welcomed them each morning with open arms, and that sent them home in the afternoons having met success at some point during the course of the day. I was encountering professionals who felt burnt out and discouraged. Many of my conversations with them were dominated by negative comments about being teachers or about the lack of funding or whatever else. Listening to these once-gifted teachers and administrators I couldn't help but feel that they had worked tirelessly each day and year, yet they felt that very little appreciation had been given to them for their efforts. Very few had ever been told "Thank You" or "Good Job." At this point I realized that I was in the right place. As a leader this was my strength. After a period of time there is very little intrinsic affirmation after breaking up fights, getting cursed out by a parent, or covering a class for the second straight day. A good leader must always affirm and validate the staff.

As each day passed I realized that I had a wonderful opportunity for hiring and placing teachers in front of children who would become a part of their life-long memories. I will never forget the feeling I had after making my first selection. I was in a meeting with other administrators and I listened intently as a vice principal made comments about the teaching and learning processes. At that moment I knew that I wanted this person to be a part of the quality team we would assemble. She did become a part of our team and, like I had always known, she did a great job. We followed a rigorous schedule for the next few months attempting to find the very best teachers and support staff we could find. A month before school was to begin we were staffed at ninety percent. The staff was a mixture of veteran teachers and first-year rookies who were ready and inspired to make a positive difference in the lives of children. I felt really good about the staff that I would lead and work with to bring about change in our district and in the attitudes of our children. What we had before us would definitely be a challenge of knowns and unknowns. One distinct advantage was that we all believed in each other and our unique abilities to capture young people.

Opening a new school was an exciting adventure. Building a team to work toward one vision and mission took total concentration and focus on everyone's part. One of the first things we did was a *needs assessment* to determine our needs as a staff. Because we were entering a school designed with technology beyond the reach of many of America's schools and certainly beyond anything we had experienced in the past, we focused on technology as our first priority and teaming as our second. Because we were operating during the summer, many of our training dates occurred before teacher contract dates. Therefore, we needed to find money to pay teachers for coming in for staff development during their summer vacations. Fortunately, a budget had been built in as we had forecasted our needs. Eighty-five percent of our teachers were able to complete our training module. This was critical as we entered our new school.

During the planning year of this project I was able to visit different school districts to see what they were doing in areas such as technology, differentiation of instruction, and authentic assessment. I was very grateful to these districts because they provided a starting point for us in terms of best practices research. By visiting, I was able to receive hard data directly from the sources. I decided that we should concentrate on building strong teams, believing that teamwork would get us through the tough times that we would surely face at different junctures along the way. After developing our teams we could also continue to focus on the continuous cycle of technology training needed to move forward.

The greatest accomplishments in life are not achieved by individuals alone, but by proactive people pulling together for a common good. Look behind every winner and you will find a great coach. Look in front of every superstar and you will see a positive role model. Look alongside every great achiever and you will find caring people offering encouragement, support, and assistance. Rising to a level of interdependent thinking would be challenging and difficult for us. The hardest part for many was to look beyond self and to ask for help when it was necessary. Our mission was to offer our gifts to benefit one another, to create mutual gain. At the center of every high-performance team is a common purpose, a mission that rises above and beyond each of the individual team members. Effective team players understand that personal issues and personality differences are secondary to team demands. This does not mean abandoning who you are or giving up your individuality. It means sharing strengths and differences to move the team forward. Building trust and creating synergy is the power of teamwork.

As we moved through this process, we asked ourselves:

1) What is our overall mission/vision?

2) What is our game plan?

3) What is expected of each team member?

4) How can each member contribute most effectively?

5) What constraints will hold the team together?

6) What constraints will break the team apart?

We wanted high performance team members who were willing to put the team first and to operate in that mode in an effective manner. This mode required everyone to lead and everyone to follow at different times. It creates a powerful dynamic that invites proactive leadership. We lead when we have something important to say or contribute, using persuasion and influence to benefit the team. We follow when others are leading or when we have a plan in place. What part of the load are you carrying? What special gifts, talents and competencies are you offering? To what extent are you leading and following effectively? What is your contribution?

Synergy grows out of diversity. Bringing people together and encouraging a free exchange of ideas and feelings enriches the decision-making process. It affords us an opportunity to create ownership in whatever we're working toward. The more involvement we have with the people in our organizations, the more ownership we have. People try harder to make it work because they are personally involved.

Stephen G. Peters

My vision is that good schools are possible for all children when we begin and end each school year with the question, "What is in the best interests of our students?"

Chapter 7

The Gentlemen's Club

The Gentlemen's Club was developed to
serve as a lifeline for saving young men from
falling through the cracks. We wanted to
have a model for demonstrating to these
students that there is another way to live.

At every professional conference, educators
talk about "at risk students" and those who
are slipping through the cracks. For some
students, it seems that the edges of those
cracks may have been greased a little. For
African-American males, however, the cracks
have become gaping holes. While our prisons
and our graveyards are filled with young
African-American males, their presence in
honor societies and institutions of higher
learning is quite noticeably lacking. Many

such young men have never really been given a chance. They have been so caught up in street life that they have never known that a different way of life exists for them. Their circumstances have taken away any prospect of having a full life, a meaningful and successful life.

The student body at Lafayette-Winona Middle School in Norfolk, Virginia, counted many such young men among its ranks. The lives that these young African-American men currently lead will play a very strong role in determining the life pattern that they will be destined to follow unless there is intervention that offers them an opportunity for something better. After our teachers, administrators, and community leaders bonded together to ensure that the school grounds were safe and that something positive was taking place in each classroom every day, the image of the school began to improve. However, after two years, we were still not reaching our *at risk* male students. I noticed a group of African-American males whom we were not capturing. We weren't even close! I felt that they could take over the school at any time.

We could always suspend these problem students, but that would not solve the problem; it would merely change its location from the school to the streets.

We developed *The Gentlemen's Club* to serve as a lifeline to save these young men from falling through the cracks. The Gentlemen's Club would demonstrate to students that there was another way to live their lives. It would prove to them that one needs not allow the rhythm of the streets to dictate the tunes that they will sing all of their lives. The Lafayette-Winona faculty decided that they needed something to compensate for the sage advice from father figures which so many troubled students lacked. These young men needed mentors—someone to give them reasons to hope for something more. Through teacher and staff recommendations, a list of young men in need of such a program was compiled.

You can imagine the types of students whose names appeared on the list of "nominees." They ranged from class cutters and smokers to gang members and felons. Their disciplinary records included poor attendance, disrespect, insubordination, harassment, hitting, profanity, disruption, fighting, and assault. Eventually, the list was narrowed to 25 young men who probably would have appeared in every teacher's "Rogues' Gallery." The team of faculty members who had volunteered to work with the Gentlemen's Club had their work cut out for them. Fortunately, more help than they ever imagined was headed their way.

In college, most of us read the now-classic, *Dress for Success*, and we knew how much appearance influenced people's impressions, especially their first impressions. A crisp white shirt and a necktie can make a remarkable change in one's appearance and in the perceptions of others. Most of our young men had neither a white shirt, a necktie, or the financial resources to acquire them. Through the efforts of our teachers and the Norfolk community, the principal's office was soon flooded with shirts, neckties, and sports coats of every size, shape, and color imaginable. For a while, it appeared that we were transforming our offices and conference rooms into men's clothing outlets!

After our community had supplied us with white shirts, with a great deal of effort and an equal amount of spray starch, Verdonda Wright, our Fine and Practical Arts Department Chairperson, transformed them into *crisp* white shirts. She also developed a handbook of etiquette and conducted "manners workshops" with our club members. "There is never an excuse for bad manners," became our rallying cry. Horatio Douglas, the club's faculty adviser, explained the fine points of knotting a necktie. Thanks to the efforts of our school family, on Mondays, our 25 selected young men would be wearing white shirts and neckties.

Fortunately, when we unveiled our gentlemen on that first Monday, a reporter for the *Virginian-Pilot* was visiting our school.

The next morning, his article on the front page of the Metro Section informed our community about the project. The school was inundated with phone calls and E-mail messages from throughout Norfolk and the surrounding cities. All of the calls were positive. Most of the callers asked, "How can I help?" Within the week, two local television stations had aired stories about the program on the evening news. *Portfolio Magazine,* a weekly local news and entertainment tabloid, did a follow-up story. Our quiet little project was starting to take on a life of its own.

In the days that followed, the letters and comments poured in.

"How wonderful!"

"Nice article. Saw it. Really loved it."

"Great idea."

"This must be an answer to a prayer. So many have been praying for our young people."

Many of the writers enclosed checks. One contributor wrote:

"Gentlemen's Club members, I hope these donations help you to achieve your worthy goals. Education will make you strong and respected."

We had community support, and it wasn't just from the African-American community. The entire Hampton Roads area pitched in with support.

The owner of *Il Porto,* an exclusive downtown restaurant, invited the club members to his restaurant for dinner. For most of the young men, this represented their first experience to dine in a Five Star restaurant. Again, the school's faculty lined up in support. It seemed that even before the call for help went out, it was already arriving. Jean Bankos and George Felt, two staff members, volunteered to chauffeur the club members to the restaurant in their family vans. Faculty adviser Douglas was still knotting neckties when the vans of anxious gentlemen arrived at the restaurant.

During the dinner real cooperative learning and authentic assessment was witnessed. The young men displayed splendid manners. More than a few eyebrows were raised when "Dusty," a 240-pound neighborhood tough guy, began explaining to (the appropriately-named) "Bruiser" and "Snoop" the intricacies of unfolding a napkin and proper positioning of the left arm while dining. Assessing the success of Mrs. Wright's dining lesson by the performance of the gentlemen, Dusty commented, "Everybody at Lafayette-Winona knows, she don't play games." Smiling, he then turned to a staff member to discuss the distinctions between a dinner fork and a salad fork.

Other community groups donated items to the club as well. We received items like tickets to college basketball games and theater presentations. Both the Hampton Roads Black Banker's Association and the Hampton Roads Black Attorney's Association volunteered to organize a one-on-one mentorship program for the members of the club. The Norfolk

Police Department organized a day-long problem-solving seminar for the school.

Tony Brothers, an NBA referee, heard about the club and adopted not only our gentlemen, but the entire school. As often as his busy season schedule allowed, he tutored, mentored, and coached Lafayette-Winona Middle School students. Brothers wears the number 56 on his official's jersey, but he soon became number 1 in the hearts of the students at Lafayette-Winona Middle School. Through his efforts 32 students (many of them members of the Gentlemen's Club) were able to take a trip to Landover, Maryland, to watch the Washington *Wizards* play at the U.S. Air Arena. He also arranged for a pizza feast before the game.

The Norfolk Redevelopment and Housing Authority supplied the bus and the driver for the 500-mile round trip. While we were in the Washington, D.C., area, we made time for the students to spend a few hours in the Smithsonian Museum. Most of our students were already "street smart" we wanted them to be "book smart" too. The project began at Lafayette-Winona Middle School but a little publicity has rendered an outpouring of support that has made the Gentlemen's Club the property of the entire Hampton Roads (Norfolk and beyond) area.

Caring and concern must be a two-way street. As our community gave to the Gentlemen's Club we realized that the club's members had to start giving back to the community that was supporting them. Lafayette-Winona's community service was initiated within the walls of the school. The members of the Gentlemen's Club began their service as cafeteria monitors and ushers at school assemblies. Soon they were involved in a neighborhood clean up project. Although litter no longer had a chance, our young men suddenly did.

Their efforts expanded into convalescent homes and hospitals. A letter-writing project with senior citizens developed prompting this response from an 83-year-old great-grandmother, "It's just wonderful to see how these young people care. I do so look forward to their letters each week." The Gentlemen's Club also organized a mentoring program with students at Campostella Elementary School. Our young men were giving as well as receiving. Our community was beginning to draw some returns on its investment. Young men who were once destined to be future criminals had been transformed into positive role models for younger children.

It's amazing what can happen when you take a chance, when you become a risk taker. The superintendent often encouraged teachers and administrators to become risk takers. His reaction came even before others in Hampton Roads: "Norfolk Public Schools is proud of your newsworthy accomplishment. Keep up the good work!" The Gentlemen's Club, became a win-win situation. Most of our young men had never experienced any measure of success. In the classroom, many had been placed (rather than promoted) at their current grade levels. During the previous school year many club members had failed at least half their subjects; several had failed all seven of their classes. First-quarter report cards revealed a much different result, a much improved product. Of our 27 students, 15 had passed seven of their classes; seven students had passed six of their classes; and the others had passed either four or five classes. Three members of the club actually made the Honor Roll. In any school, and even more so in an inner-city school, these were significant academic gains.

Better grades were a reflection of increased attendance, improved behavior and social skills. Compared to their attendance during the previous school year, these young men had improved their attendance by almost 8 percent. Disciplinary referrals, conduct notices, and suspensions were greatly reduced during the first quarter of school. Susan Bechtol, eighth grade Dean of Students, explained the decline in disciplinary action by saying, "Each of these young men have been given a reason for wanting to be here. As I watch them each day, many are changing for the better. You can see it in their actions and their attitudes toward others."

Through the knowing eyes of a veteran teacher, Frances Washington, the project was given this assessment: "What began as one man's dream has become a model of what school and community can do once they come together." A respected teacher and teacher's association officer stated, "The Gentlemen's Club provides an opportunity for young men to serve as positive role models for their peers and for younger students while building their own self-esteem and confidence." Jo-Ann Bashay, seventh grade Dean of Students, perhaps sums up the entire project best: "We have managed, with lots of encouragement from the community, to mold disruptive students into GENTLEMEN." Our staff was so pleased with the early results of the project that they established a *Ladies' Club* for our young women. One good idea often leads to another.

As test scores came in, we had made major strides on functional- and performance-based tests. We also had more minority students to enroll in foreign language classes and other more rigorous courses. One year later, the distinction of *Virginia Blue Ribbon School* was bestowed upon Lafayette-Winona Middle School. Hard work, dedication, reciprocal respect, vision, and strong beliefs go a long way when you prepare the culture for change. The consistent process and structure of the Gentlemen's Club is aided by the Goals, Code of Conduct, Weekly Progress Reports, a point system, and other incentives.

The Gentlemen's Club Code of Conduct and many of the instructional activities have been adapted from Mychal Wynn's book, *Empowering African-American Males to Succeed: A Ten-Step Approach for Parents and Teachers.*

Gentlemen's Club Code of Conduct

1. We will begin each day by affirming our individual and collective greatness.

2. We will begin each day by giving each other a hug (or a handshake).

3. We will always do our best to help each other to achieve their goals and dreams.

4. We will always strive for the highest character, integrity, and honesty.

5. We will always maintain a passion for excellence in whatever we do. Anything worth doing is worth doing well!

6. We will always maintain the manners and posture worthy of a royal heritage, carrying ourselves with pride and dignity.

7. We will always demonstrate respect for ourselves and for the rights and property of others.

8. We will never say negative or discouraging things to one another.

9. We will never hit each other.

10. We will apply each of the first nine codes of conduct to our lives as though someone is always watching.

Gentlemen's Club Pledge

Today I pledge to be
    the best me that I can be,
    to demonstrate integrity in all that I do,
    to treat others with respect,
    remembering always that I must
    respect myself first.

Today I pledge that I, and I alone,
    am responsible for making
    good choices.

Today I pledge to demonstrate those
    behaviors that are consistent with
    following my own dreams and
    aspirations.

Today I pledge to be grateful for this
    opportunity to be led by those
    I admire.

Gentlemen's Club Weekly Progress Report

Student Name: _____

Date: _____   Period: _____

Subject/Class

_____

Absences: _____   Tardiness: _____

Behavior

Please circle:
Excellent   Good   Average   Needs Improvement

Comments: _____

_____

_____

Classwork/Classroom Participation

Please circle:
Excellent   Good   Average   Needs Improvement

Comments: _____

_____

_____

Teacher Advisory Signature

_____

Gentlemen's Club Goals

- Carry oneself in a gentlemanly manner.

- Progress academically.

- Learn to make better choices.

- Improve behavior.

- Set personal goals. Work hard to achieve those goals.

- Set new goals.

- Avoid suspensions.

- Take responsibility for one's actions.

- Become a productive member of society.

Each gentlemen's club member was taught basic etiquette and how to tie a tie.

The Basics

Etiquette (et-uh-kt): *The prescribed forms and practices of correct behavior.*

In the 1880's a definition for good manners (which is still acceptable) was "Intelligent kindness, based on consideration for other people rather than ourselves."

Meals (family or in public) should be pleasurable occasions. The following items are a basic guide to follow to make mealtime pleasant and enjoyable for everyone:

A. Arrive promptly for meals. Never keep the host/hostess waiting. This will ensure that food is served at the appropriate temperature.

B. Be considerate about helping with before and after meal chores. Don't just excuse yourself from the table, leaving your dishes (unless you are in a restaurant). Be sure to clean up after yourself. (It will go a long way in receiving more invitations to eat out!)

C. It is considered rude to not participate in table conversation. Share in, and be attentive to the subject of conversation. *Don't concentrate on problems or bring up unpleasant topics.*

D. Mealtime should not be a time to rush or be anxious. Relax and enjoy your food, family, and/or friends.

E. **Never** blow your nose at the table. Excuse yourself to the restroom if you must.

F. If you have to sneeze or cough, cover your nose and mouth with your napkin and turn your head away from the table.

G. When chewing food, keep your mouth closed. Nothing looks more unpleasant than someone at another table (or the one where you are sitting) with food coming out of his/her mouth.

H. **<u>Please</u>**, do not talk with food in your mouth. Whatever you have to say can wait until you have swallowed your food and cleared your mouth. If you absolutely have to say something, gracefully place your napkin in front of your mouth when you speak.

I. Your eyes should not be bigger than your stomach. If you put the food on your plate, eat it. It is unfair to your parent, host, or hostess for you to waste food.

J. Bring the fork up to your mouth to eat. Don't bring your head down to the plate or bowl.

K. Eat with poise. Don't shovel the food into your mouth as though you have never eaten before.

L. Do not blow on food to cool it.

M. Cut a few pieces of food at a time.

Don't cut it all up at once.

N. Break off and butter a small piece of bread at a time. Do not butter the whole piece and bite off of it.

O. Use serving utensils to serve yourself, not your own flatware.

P. Open your napkin, fold it in half, and lay it across your lap.

Q. Before getting up from the table while others are still eating, say, "Excuse me, please."

R. Remove seeds (such as from watermelon or grapes) from your mouth with a spoon. Never spit them out.

S. **Never** comb or brush your hair at the table.

T. Always pass food on a serving plate.

U. When you have finished eating, your napkin should be placed beside your plate, not balled up in your plate.

V. A gentleman always stands when a lady approaches or leaves the table.

Four Course Semi-formal

Each Gentlemen's Club member actually sat through a four course semi-formal dinner which included a formal table setting.

Eating Styles

American Style

The fork is held in the left hand with the tines down. The knife is held in the right hand only to cut the food.

After the food is cut, the knife is placed on the edge of the plate, the cutting edge of the knife should face the center of the plate. The fork is returned to the right hand to eat. This process is repeated until you have finished cutting your food.

Continental (or European) Style

A right-handed person holds the knife in the right hand and the fork in the left hand. Food is cut and eaten without changing hands. This style is easier and becoming more popular with American executives.

Resting Position

When you have stopped eating for a period of time (maybe to go to the restroom) you should leave your flatware in the resting position. This alerts the waiter or waitress that you have not yet finished and your plate will not be taken away. The tines of the fork are down resting over the blade of the knife .

Deadly Disasters and How to Handle Them

Even though you try hard to be careful, occasionally, an accident occurs at the dinner table. Don't laugh, run out of the room, or apologize twenty times. These things do happen. If things don't always go the way that you had hoped...STAY CALM.

Now suppose:

A. *Your hostess has served you something that you are allergic to.* Don't make a scene. Simply say, "No, thank you, I don't care for any."

B. *You burp at the table (or someone else does):* DON'T LAUGH! Simply say, "Excuse me" and don't bring attention to yourself. Keep your mouth closed and if possible cover your mouth with your napkin (it helps to keep the sound muffled).

C. *You are dining at someone's home or in a restaurant and you see a foreign object in your food (a bug or hair):* DON'T YELL, "Gross!" Simply bring it to the waiter's (or waitress') attention (it will be replaced). If at someone's home, quietly mention it to the hostess.

D. *Eating Chicken:* Do not pick it up with your fingers unless you are at a picnic.

E. *Eating Corn-on-the-Cob:* You may securely hold both ends with your fingers and eat.

F. *Eating Spaghetti:* A small amount of spaghetti should be picked up with the fork and wound using a spoon for assistance. Spaghetti should never be slurped up into your mouth from the plate.

G. *Eating Soup:* Let the soup cool naturally. Don't blow it. The soup spoon should be worked away from you and not toward you when eating. Never pick the bowl up to pour those last drops into your mouth.

Believe it or not, our Gentlemen Club members not only eagerly and actively participated in the table etiquette sessions they prided themselves on becoming "cultured!"

Chapter 8

Most Often Asked Questions about the Gentlemen's Club

The Gentlemen's Club process is easily adaptable to fit the needs of most school communities and has a sister component, The Ladies' Club for young ladies.

— Lisa Vernon, Social Worker
Centennial High School, Champagne, IL

In this chapter, I will answer the most commonly asked questions about the Gentlemen's Club and its process. Remember that our Gentlemen's Club reflected an intervention strategy that evolved from the core questions, "What is in the best interests of our students?" and, "What must we do to achieve our vision?"

Q. What age group is targeted by programs like the Gentlemen's Club?

A. Grades 4 and 5 on the elementary level and all middle and high school students.

Q. Who would run a program like the Gentlemen's Club?

A. In our situation we ran our Gentlemen's Club through the efforts of teachers and support personnel. However, such programs can be successfully implemented through churches, communities, and Boy's and Girl's Clubs.

Q. What type of costs are involved in implementing an intervention strategy like the Gentlemen's Club?

A. Program facilitators would have to be trained (e.g., how to work with confrontational students, effective cross-gender cross-ethnic communi-cation, and the unique cultural and demographic framework of the families and communities of those students being served, etc.). A budget for rewards and incentives should also be established.

Q. Can such a process be used for other ethnic or gender groups?

A. Yes. Keep in mind that this is a process for dealing with the unique needs of students. We established our initial Gentlemen's Club for our targeted population, African-American Males.

Q. How should the participants be selected?

A. Review your school's data to determine the pattern of need unique to your school community. Some of the indicators include, but are not limited to, attendance, suspensions, office referrals, academic achievement, performance on standardized testing, and attitudes toward school.

Q. **Who should work with the groups?**

A. Consider two facilitators, highly developed in Interpersonal Intelligence and who can make a cultural or gender connection with students, for each group of 15 - 20 students.

Q. **How often should the groups meet?**

A. A good time frame is once a week for an hour and a half. Consider an additional one and a half hour recreational day per week to be used as an incentive for those who are "doing the right thing," while others are involved in tutorial sessions.

Q. **What should participants do when they meet?**

A. Participants should be led by the club's facilitators through weekly modules designed to deal with the unique needs of your school community. Some modules might deal with study skills while others might deal with social skills. We developed the Gentlemen's Club curriculum for our school by adapting instructional activities from various sources that met the unique needs of our students. Among the materials that we used were Mychal Wynn's books, *The Eagles who Thought They were Chickens, Empowering African-American Males to Succeed,* and *The Eagle Team Leadership Curriculum.*

Q. **How do we ensure that this process works for our students?**

A. The key to success is the facilitators—people with a personal passion to help children and a deep-rooted belief that they can truly make a difference in the lives of young people.

Q. **What kind of hard data do you have to support the apparent success of your Gentlemen's Club?**

A. Of our first 18 participants, 12 are in college and 4 are in the military. Last year, a Maryland Chapter sent 21 of 22 eighth graders to high school without them having to attend summer school. Attendance is up, office referrals are down, and suspensions are down consistently at each of the chapters established since we began the first chapter at our middle school.

Q. **Who will benefit and how?**

A. The benefits are reaped by the schools, the community, the families, and the children.

Q. **Will we need additional staff to run this type of program?**

A. No additional staff is required.

Q. **Is active parent involvement necessary?**

A. Active involvement by parents is always a plus, however, as is the case with other school-based programs (e.g., athletic, band, cheerleading, etc.) the facilitators (or coaches) have tremendous influence over the success of the young people involved.

Q. **What do the participants seem to like the most about the process?**

A. The participants appear to like the structure, success, rewards, meeting new acquaintances, the academic success, and the overall experience.

Q. **What is the ultimate goal of the program?**

A. The ultimate goals of the program are to restore hope, to identify dreams and aspirations, to redirect talent and energy, to promote high academic achievement, and to produce productive members of society.

Chapter 9

The Gentlemen's Club
Goes Everywhere

The Oprah Winfrey show aired a segment
on the Gentlemen's Club and it touched us
deeply. It gave us hope for helping those in
need of help so badly.

— Freddie & Lisa Vernon
Champagne, IL

There are many wonderful things going on
with our Ladies' and Gentlemen's Clubs in
St. Mary's County. You are a gift.

— Bonnie Elward, Executive Director
Tomorrow's Child, Inc.

Children enter our schools on a daily basis
seeking solutions to many different problems.
We are given the responsibility for educating,
to the best of our abilities, those sent to us. To

accomplish this, we must continue to conceptualize operational strategies designed to fulfill our vision which often require that we develop and use effective specialized programs. A Maryland Chapter of The Gentlemen's Club was formed as a means of being proactive with a group of highly at risk males. The same holds true for the creation of the Ladies' Club and other special programs. Instead of these youngsters continuing to be suspended, we found a way to give them ownership of their future and make them a part of the solution. More times than not, our students have answers to many of the problems we face in society and in schools. We simply need to take the time to form relationships with them and to listen to them. Many specialized programs work because children have helped to develop the vision driving the programs.

In public education today we have a tendency to think that if it doesn't cost a lot of money and require a lot of time and personnel it's not worth it. There are young people who will tell you that you are wrong! Many programs require optimism, and people who care, who refuse to give up on children. A colleague once told me, "Don't give up one minute before the miracle happens." We begin things and we do not give them the time to develop to a point of effectiveness or to a point where we can evaluate their effectiveness. Promising programs are often discarded before we gather and effectively assess all pertinent data. If we assess our needs and include our students in the process of moving from problem to solution, we will find ourselves closer to solving those problems and moving on to a deeper level of teaching and learning.

Our schools cannot survive without special programs and incentives for certain students whom we are held responsible for educating. These students do not come to school ready or eager to learn. Many of them see school as a place for recreation, where they can socialize and eat two solid meals five times a week. They are not there to learn. As

I talk to students, many of them say, "Why should I keep trying? I don't do anything but fail." What insight this has given to me and my teachers! We had to build in success for our students. The more they experienced, the more they wanted to experience. Understanding this simple but important piece of information is critical to the success of any program. It provides us with clarity and purpose. The continued success of any specialized program or initiative depends upon continually revisiting what we're doing and whether it is in the best interest of our students.

Our Gentlemen's Club was featured on "The Oprah Winfrey Show," as well as in a documentary called, "America, America," which was broadcast to two million viewers in Brazil and Portugal. Due to the national exposure created by these two broadcasts, we have received hundreds of requests from the West Coast to the East Coast to help schools and communities set up Gentlemen and Ladies Clubs. We have now expanded to twenty certified sites and are growing every day. The amazing success of the Gentlemen and Ladies Clubs has come about as a result of understanding our needs and not making excuses for being unable to meet them. We didn't have money, we couldn't hire additional staff, but we weren't going to continue putting our kids out of school. We're deeply touched that something so simple has changed and will continue to change lives and restore hope to thousands of children, communities, and families.

In today's society, change is inevitable. The lack of parental involvement in America's schools is one of those changes. In traditional families of the past, the roles of the mother and father were very clear. They tended to be involved in their children's schools. Parents helped their children with homework after school. P.T.A. meetings were on the family calendar as an event that was not to be missed. Today, in many households of our public schools, children do not have fathers. Mom is there, working two jobs to make ends meet and the children are home alone more times than not. Many of society's issues stem from the breakdown of the family that once provided the structure and value system by which we all lived.

Many children in schools today are the products of a union that did not last and that did not lead to matrimony. Don't get me wrong, many children from single family homes are some of the most well-adjusted children I've ever met. However, they are the exceptions, not the rule. A large percentage of our students come to school with negative attitudes and no goals. Life seems to have dealt them a bad hand. That is why we, as educators, have to make a difference in the lives of those whom we come into contact with each day.

For schools to be successful at any level, there must be some semblance of parental involvement and support. There will, however, be situations where realistically, this will not happen. In those cases, schools have to substitute as parents. There is no other choice if we want our children to truly be successful. When there is a parent conference and no parent, someone on the staff at the school must step in as an advocate for the student. When there is a sports activity, a student with no parental support needs a representative from the school to be there for support. Eventually, these students will get the message: Someone cares about them! Our children often struggle with self-hatred because they cannot understand why the adults in their lives don't take better care of them. The word "trust" is not in their vocabularies. We must capture and restore hope to these young people!

We need to build in the involvement of parents who are actively involved in our schools and we need to do whatever is necessary for the other students. The fact that their parents aren't actively involved should not and must not be a reason for us to fail them. We must consciously reach out to all students. Over the past seventeen years, I have met and worked with some of the most caring educators in the world. There is nothing that they wouldn't do to positively impact the lives of children. We are called to be that which we are needed to be in each one of our children's lives on a daily basis. We are called to teach whether a child's parent is present or not. We must always stay focused on our vision and remain true to our mission: To educate our students. . . ALL STUDENTS.

Epilogue

How Will I Overcome?

How will I overcome?
I will overcome by reaching back,
remembering with precision
those obstacles others overcame.

How will I overcome?
I will overcome with
the help of others who
have shown me they really care.

How will I overcome?

I will overcome

by constantly telling myself that

my future is bright

if I work hard each and every day.

How will I overcome?

I will overcome

by remembering that

failure is NOT an option.

References

Covey, Stephen R. *The Seven Habits of Highly Effective People.* NY: Simon & Schuster, 1989.

Fallan & Boyer. *The New Meaning of Educational Change.* http://www.effectiveschools.com, 1991.

Fallan & Hargreaves. *Successful School Improvement.* http://www.effectiveschools.com, 1992.

Hoving, Walter and Eula, Joe. *Tiffany's Table Manners for Teenagers.* NY: Random House, 1989.

Inc. Magazine. *The New Commandments of Change.* June 1999.

Kozol, Jonathan. *Amazing Grace: The Lives of Children and The Conscience of a Nation.* NY: Crown Publishers, 1995.

Mallory, John T. *Dress for Success.* NY: Warner Books, 1993.

Okwu, Julian C.R. *Face Forward: Young African American Men in a Critical Age.* San Francisco, CA: Chronicle Books, 1997.

Peters, Stephen G. *The Gentlemen's Club Curriculum Guide.* Salisbury, MD: Peters & Associates, 2000.

Portfolio Magazine. *Principal turning At-Risk Youth into Gentlemen.* Fall 1996.

Virginian–Pilot. *Gentlemen's Club: Turning Problems into Princes.* October 1996.

Wynn, Mychal. *Empowering African-American Males To Succeed: A Ten Step Approach for Parents and Teachers.* Marietta, GA: Rising Sun Publishing, 1992.

Wynn, Mychal. *Increasing Student Achievement: Volume I Vision.* Marietta, GA: Rising Sun Publishing, 2001.

Wynn, Mychal. *The Eagle Team: A Leadership Curriculum.* Marietta, GA: Rising Sun Publishing, 2001.

Wynn, Mychal. *The Eagles who Thought They were Chickens: A Tale of Discovery.* Marietta, GA: Rising Sun Publishing, 1993.

For information regarding
establishing a Gentlemen's Club or
to arrange for Stephen Peters to
speak to your school or
organization contact:

Visionary Leaders Institute:

http://www.VLI123.com

(800) 223.4244

Other books from
Rising Sun Publishing

Building Dreams: Elementary Ed. Teacher's Guide
(ISBN 1-880463-45-9 • $29.95)

An indispensible resource tool for elementary and middle school teachers. Lessons and activities help teachers to develop more effective parent communication and a more positive classroom climate and culture.

Building Dreams: Helping Students Discover Their Potential: Teacher, Parent, Mentor Workbook
(ISBN 1-880463-42-3 • $9.95)

Guides teachers, parents, and mentors through exercises for facilitating discussion and direction for a student or group of students. Mentors learn how to move beyond the rhetoric of lecturing to meaningful and relevant dialogue; dialogue that will facilitate bonding and that will help students focus on long-term outcomes.

Don't Quit
(ISBN 1-880463-26-1 • $9.95)

Mychal Wynn's critically-acclaimed book of poetry contains 26 poems of inspiration and affirmation. Each verse is complemented by an inspiring quotation.

Follow Your Dreams: Lessons That I Learned in School
(ISBN 1-880463-51-2 • $7.95)

All students are confronted with choices during their school-aged years, from kindergarten through college. Which group do I identify with? How seriously do I take my schoolwork? How important is it to establish goals? What are my dreams and aspirations? How can my time in school help me to achieve them?

Mychal Wynn shares his story about the lessons that he learned while grappling with such questions and how he became a high academic achiever along the road to discovering his dreams and aspirations.

Empowering African-American Males to Succeed: A Ten-Step Approach for Parents and Teachers
Book (ISBN 1-880463-01-6 • $15.95)
Teacher/Parent Workbook (ISBN 1-880463-02-4 • $9.95)

African-American males are the most "at-risk" students in America's schools. They are the most likely to be placed into special education, drop out of school, be suspended, be the victims or perpetrators of violent crimes, or be incarcerated. This book outlines a clear, cohesive set of strategies to turn the tide of underachievement to personal empowerment.

Enough is Enough: The Explosion in Los Angeles
(ISBN 1-880463-34-2 • $9.95)

Provides an introspective analysis of the problems strangling those who live in America's urban battle zones and moves the reader toward solutions to help urban America help itself before it's too late.

Increasing Student Achievement: Volume I: Vision
(ISBN 1-880463-10-5 • $29.95)

Every school community is undergoing the continuous transformation cycle. Whatever the levels of student achievement, standardized test scores, truancy, absenteeism or suspensions, each school is driven by its vision or established goals. This, the first volume of the *Increasing Student Achievement* series outlines how to develop your school's vision; how to develop a core team for carrying out the vision; how to develop guiding beliefs and core values to lead the way toward achieving the vision; and how to create operational strategies so that the vision becomes more than rhetoric.

Ten Steps to Helping Your Child Succeed in School: Volume I
(ISBN 1-880463-50-4 • $9.95)

Outlines easy-to-follow steps for parents and teachers to better understand children so that we can better direct them. The steps help parents and teachers to easily identify a child's personality types, learning styles, Multiple Intelligences, best and worst learning situations, dreams and aspirations.

Test of Faith: A Personal Testimony of God's Grace, Mercy, and Omnipotent Power
(ISBN 1-880463-09-1 • $9.95)

"This book has become more than a recalling of my hospital experiences, it has become a testimony of the power of the human spirit; a testimony of the healing power of the Holy Spirit; and ultimately a personal testimony of my relationship with God, my belief in His anointing, and my trust in His power, grace, and mercy."

The Eagle Team: Leadership Curriculum
Student Guide (ISBN 1-880463-16-4 • $19.95)
Facilitator's Guide (ISBN 1-880463-39-3 • $29.95)

An effective intervention and leadership program designed to help unlock the passion within students by leading them through a series of units that will help them to discover their dreams and aspirations as they develop the leadership and academic skills to be recognized as leaders within their respective school communities.

The Eagles who Thought They were Chickens:
A Tale of Discovery
Book (ISBN 1-880463-12-1 • $4.95)
Student Activity Book (ISBN 1-880463-19-9 • $5.95)
Teacher's Guide (ISBN 1-880463-18-0 • $9.95)

Chronicles the journey of a great eagle; historically perched at the right hand of the great king in her native Africa; captured and taken aboard a slave ship; and her eggs that are eventually hatched, and their struggles in the chicken yard where they are scorned and ridiculed for their differences. The story offers parallels to behaviors in classrooms and on school playgrounds where children are teased by schoolyard "chickens" and bullied by schoolyard "roosters."

Visit our web site for a complete
listing of our books, materials,
and training programs:
http://www.rspublishing.com
or call for a free catalog
(800) 524-2813